GLASS
HOUSES

GLASS HOUSES

Φ

TOWARD A HARMONY BETWEEN ARCHITECTURE AND NATURE

Indeed, we should strive to bring nature, houses, and people together into a higher unity. When you see nature through the glass walls of Farnsworth House, it gets a deeper meaning than [from] outside. More is asked for from nature, because it becomes a part of a larger whole.[1]

LUDWIG MIES VAN DER ROHE

Widely recognized as one of the most influential architects of the twentieth century, Ludwig Mies van der Rohe designed buildings characterized by a Modernist aesthetic that emphasizes simplicity, transparency, and a sense of open spaciousness. Running throughout his work is the idea of a higher spiritual harmony between architecture and nature, and each project in this book speaks to that belief. While the program of a house can be a simple problem to solve architecturally, the number and range of solutions reflects countless ways of life. Assembled here are fifty modern and contemporary homes that use glass to enclose and support human habitation.

GLASS WALLS, ENCLOSURE, AND STRUCTURE

Every house in this book seeks to redefine enclosure by creating spaces with large areas of glass, from translucent walls as in Pierre Chareau and Bernard Bijvoet's Maison de Verre (see pp.122–5) to the geometric volumes in Arrhov Frick's Viggsö (see pp.178–81). From delicate structural frames inside and outside in Santiago Valdivieso and Stefano Rolla's Engawa House (see pp.60–5) to sculptural enclosures in Design Haus Liberty's Villa Mosca Bianca (see pp.108–13), these projects question how space-defining enclosure is separated and connected from inside to outside. By rethinking and articulating opaque load-bearing walls into transparent load-bearing and non-load-bearing walls, these buildings frame new relationships with nature and landscape. By separating and connecting structure from spatial enclosure, the featured glass houses build on Mies's Modernist development of the skeletal structural frame while providing thermal comfort and protection from the elements.

PICTORIAL FRAME

Within each project, the extensive use of glass creates a sense of transparency and openness that pictorially frames the views of the surrounding rural and urban landscapes in unique and powerful ways. Prussian architect Karl Friedrich Schinkel (1781–1841) developed the practice of juxtaposing near and far views to heighten the aesthetic experience of nature, and was an early influence on Mies. At the same time in art, a motif of eighteenth-century Picturesque and nineteenth-century Romantic painting was the deliberate exclusion of the middle ground. This afforded a union between architecture and landscape by editing down the expanse of scenery taken in one view, and extending the view until it overlapped and merged with the horizon. Like the vista in Michael Kendrick's Looking Glass Lodge (see pp.228–31), by dropping the middle ground and inscribing a horizontal edge connected to the vertical edges defined by trees, a framed vista is created. This works in two ways: by raising the eye and extending the distance to the horizon, and by removing or lowering any disrupting trees or bushes between viewer and vista. Other pictorial frames are defined by raised plinths, exterior terraces, extended roof overhangs, structural frames, lattice screens, and garden courtyards.

GLASS BARNS

A conventional house might be made up of four opaque walls supporting a pitched roof pierced by a chimney, with no separation between structure and enclosure. Several projects in this book reinvent the form of a barn or shed-type traditional house as a transparent object. By retaining the traditional profile, projects like Tatiana Bilbao's Los Terrenos (see pp.104–7), Nadine Engelbrecht's The Conservatory (see pp.78–81), Linda Bergroth and Ville Hara's Green Shed (see pp.40–3), and Maas Kristinsson Architecten's Villa (see pp.32–5) blend old and new, inside to outside. With relatively modest glass panel sizes and lattice-like frames, mullions and structures, the walls of these buildings continue and translate into glass roofs, creating the impression of a transparent crystal instead of an umbrella-like canopy roof structure.

EXTERIOR FRAME

Some of the projects in this book also use delicate frame structures to replace opaque load-bearing walls, their thin load-bearing columns *outside* of the glass enclosure. Projects such as Mies's Farnsworth House (see pp.66–71), RAMA estudio's Mirador House (see pp.82–5), and Helgessongonzaga's Tjurpannan House (see pp.190–3) continue the separation of space-defining enclosure from wall to structural frame and roof. Unlike the glass barns where the pitched roof is also glass and transparent, here, opaque roof planes extend and cantilever over the glass enclosure and exterior columns like the branches of a tree. In Pierre Koenig's Stahl House (see pp.182–5), this is seen in the dramatic roof and floor extensions of the exterior covered terrace. Or in Tjurpannan House with its cantilevered roof, terrace, and trellis creating what in traditional Japanese architecture is called *engawa*, or the space between inside and outside. Many of these houses feature long, low profiles that seem to stretch out toward the horizon, strengthening the connection between inside and out.

INTERIOR FRAME

In contrast, Philip Johnson's Glass House (see pp.210–15) places the load-bearing columns just inside the glass enclosure, a subtle shift that aligns it with the space-defining enclosure of the roof. In Matteo Arnone and Pep Pons's Library House (see pp.136–41), Makoto Takei + Chie Nabeshima's Square House (see pp.202–5), and Lina Bo Bardi's Glass House (see pp.98–103), the structural columns are brought even further inside away from the perimeter glass enclosure. With Square House, the interior columns are further dispersed and aggregated into a forest of columns that help define activities for living. In Christian Kerez's House with One Wall (see pp.186–9), the traditional, opaque load-bearing walls are displaced even further into a single, stacked load-bearing wall in the center of the house plan, allowing the perimeter to be opened up to enormous glass enclosures that create complete transparency between inside and outside. Like the cantilever-covered terrace in Farnsworth House, only the ceiling and floor planes create the sense of space-defining enclosure here.

FIGURAL ENCLOSURE

In modern architecture, figural enclosure is often used to create dramatic and striking designs from sculptural forms and curves that enclose and define spaces. Ryue Nishizawa's House in Los Vilos (see pp.232–7) and Anttinen Oiva's Summer House (see pp.130–5) use glass enclosures that are set back from a sculptural cantilevered roof that warps and bends in section like the surrounding distant mountains and nearby boulders. This movement creates a figural enclosure that is like being inside an arch or cave, and at the same time completely open between inside and outside. A similar figural enclosure is created with the dynamic tetrahedral roof of John Lautner's Sheats-Goldstein Residence (see pp.26–31). There, the cantilevered roof provides all of the necessary vertical and horizontal structure, allowing the glass enclosure to be free from columns and window frames. In NO ARCHITECTURE's Courtyard House (see pp.224–7), OFFICE Kersten Geers David Van Severen's Solo House II (see pp.118–21), Richard Foster's The Round House (see pp.94–7), and Herzog & de Meuron's Kramlich Residence and Collection (see pp.194–7), figural enclosures are created by curved and faceted glass enclosures in plan. In The Round House and Courtyard House, this is achieved by the faceted glass enclosures that create external circular and internal oval figures. Similarly, Kramlich Residence and Collection introduces curved and faceted glass enclosures to displace in plan the alignment of roof and glass wall with a faceted and curved figural glass enclosure below a rectilinear cantilevered roof, while Solo House II contrasts a circular roof and covered terrace with orthogonal and faceted glass enclosures.

ECOLOGICAL SOCIAL TRANSPARENCY

Located in a wide variety of climates, cultures, and contexts, these projects seek new ways to define architecture and living today. Central to this exploration is how glass creates relationships between inside and outside through material properties such as lightness, transparency, translucency, and reflectivity.

Each project sees architecture as a means of bridging the gap between people and nature, and uses glass and other transparent materials to create a sense of connection between the built environment and the surrounding landscape. Urban projects like Victorian Remix by Guarnieri Architects (see pp.44–7) and Small House by Kazuyo Sejima (see pp.150–3) also allow for continuity between inside and outside by extending the space of the interior to an exterior space or walled garden. At a variety of scales, glass transforms each house into a lens that focuses near views and far vistas of trees and forests, deserts and mountains—framing landscapes and illuminating interiors in tandem with the rhythm of day and night, and the cycle of the seasons.

By using glass, the houses in this book emphasize a connection with nature through transparent walls that blur the boundaries between inside and outside. This relationship is further amplified by continuous perimeter circulation inside, which promotes flexible and adaptable floor plans for daily living. Transparency in architecture can be said to break down the separation between open and closed, public and private, individual and collective, interior and exterior, in order to dissolve space, and allow architecture to almost disappear.

ANDREW HEID

1   Mies van der Rohe. In Christian Norberg-Schulz, "Talks with Mies van der Rohe," L'*Architecture d'aujourd'hui* 29, no.79 (September 1958): 100.

MIRROR HOUSES   2015

South Tyrol is the largest apple-growing area in Europe, the region of Bolzano alone having around 7,000 apple farms. The Mirror Houses are a pair of holiday homes for guests of the client, who lives in a restructured farmhouse on the same property, tucked in this idyllic location surrounded by mountains outside the city of Bolzano. One of the main aims was to grant full privacy to both the host and the guests, resulting in a cubic structure that hosts the two autonomous units, with a private garden and independent access. Seemingly floating above the ground, the units have a certain lightness and provide panoramic views over the orchard landscape from their cantilevered terraces. A black aluminum shell frames the building, giving it a clear definition and a contemporary appearance. The rear end and terraced front are fully glazed, with a dynamically curved, eye-like opening that leads the aluminum shell to frame the glazing on the sides of the volume. Mirrored glass has been used on the west facade, which borders with the farmhouse, providing intimacy, while allowing the units to reflect the surrounding landscape and become close to invisible at certain times of the day. The glass is laminated with a UV coating to help birds see the glass and avoid flying into it. Two large skylights have been placed on the roof to channel additional daylight into the rooms below.

LOOKOUT HOUSE   2018

Everything about this house is complex. There are no simple lines or shapes, no accessible site, and no consolidating panoramic view that can be used as a focal point. It lies in a natural reserve surrounded by ski resorts on the border of California and Nevada, in close proximity to Lake Tahoe, and at the foot of a three-million-year-old volcano. The unifying design principle was to respect this ancient site, which is defined by sloping rocky terrain featuring boulders up to 15 ft (4.5 m) wide that demand particular thought and treatment. Responding to the monumental character of the site, Lookout House has a heavy brutalist presence, impressive in the scale, plan, and space on offer. Floor-to-ceiling windows and doors lighten the decidedly muted color palette of volcanic basalt, walnut, and concrete walls and allow sunlight to pour into the interior while inviting the tall and sparse fir forest into the view. Tinted glass windows in a shade described by the architects as "cooling magma" have been installed strategically to provide warmth and unexpected highlights in this otherwise sober home environment, using light and color as a medium to stimulate emotions, in a way that is more reminiscent of an art installation than a utilitarian device.

OPTICAL GLASS HOUSE   2012

Situated in Hiroshima, one of Japan's most modern cities, Optical Glass House proposes a series of innovative solutions to the problems associated with contemporary city living. Nestled into a small plot between two tall commercial buildings, the house is subject to a vivid soundscape of road and industrial noise. To protect the daily life of their clients from the outside bustle, architects Hiroshi Nakamura & Nap designed a glass masonry wall that wraps around the full height of the building's front elevation. The 28.2 × 28.2 ft (8.6 × 8.6 m) facade comprises 6,000 borosilicate glass blocks specially cast for this purpose, weighing around 13 tons (11.8 metric tons). The blocks act as acoustic and visual cocoons, granting tranquility and privacy while allowing light to flood through the building, creating water-like reflections on the walls. The unique property of glass to separate and yet allow light to permeate is being used inventively, and this stylistic device is repeated indoors as a partition between the living room and stairwell. Between the inner and outer walls, a Japanese garden contrasts with the cold connotations of glass to create a connective, intimate space. Outside, at street level, none of this calm magic can be seen or anticipated.

SHEATS-GOLDSTEIN RESIDENCE   1963

A modernist house of historical importance, the
Sheats-Goldstein Residence is the first architectural
acquisition of the Los Angeles County Museum
of Art (LACMA). It was gifted to the museum by
its last owner, James Goldstein. The influential
residence, built primarily from glass and concrete,
is a complete work of art because the architecture,
furniture, garden, windows, lighting, and every
other detail were designed by John Lautner.
What catches the eye immediately is the perfectly
seamless transition from one glass panel to the
next. No rigid window frame disturbs the exuberant
views over Los Angeles from the office, which is
glazed on all sides and closed off by a tinted glass
panel that delicately connects the roof to the walls
with the help of minimal metal fixtures. As well as
operable glass doors and windows that appear
to float, Lautner designed functional glass furniture
that echoes the sharp angles and pitches of the
structure and projects dramatic shadows across the
interiors. The glass facades reflect the surrounding
tropical vegetation, the cityscape, and the sleek
interiors, all of which merge to create an impression
of surreal beauty with a filmic atmosphere
appropriate to the location.

VILLA 2014

This house in the Dutch province of North Brabant has been designed to build a bridge between the region's traditional style and the expectations that a contemporary country residence should fulfill. The clash of these two worlds can be seen in the classical shape of the two pitched roofs and the choice of materials, with thatch, glass, and steel coexisting. One of the two thatched volumes contains the living room, dining area, and kitchen, enclosed by glazed gables, and two bedrooms entirely closed off by black wooden cladding on the north side, which are connected to the entrance and service pavilion by a fully glazed corridor that gives the villa its H-shaped plan. The second wing features a more extravagant shape linked to its stylistic function. Imitating a greenhouse, the glazed rafters stretch beyond the thatch so that part of the roof remains uncovered to catch maximum daylight and opens to allow ventilation. Double-height glazed gables cover the living unit's maisonette floor, unifying the two wings. The large glazed panels stand out prominently against the classically flat Dutch landscape, which is captured along with the movement of the water in a rectangular pool in a series of endlessly changing reflections on the surface of the glass.

LA CLAIRIÈRE   2021

Tucked among hundred-year-old oak and
maple trees at the shore of a reservoir formed by
a dam on the Millstone River in the far northeastern
corner of Princeton, this house blends into its leafy
surroundings. Its name, "La Clairière," is French
for "the glade" and refers to the glazed centerpiece
between two black monolithic volumes. This
double-height, fully glazed "void" contains the
living area of the home, composed of kitchen and
dining spaces and an open mezzanine offering
views across the water. The double exposure of
the glass core opening onto the front and back
gardens allows its owners to witness sunrise and
sunset from the same space and enjoy abundant
natural light throughout the day. Careful siting
protects inhabitants from the heat and glare of
southern exposure. Smaller openings in the two
brick volumes, which house the bedrooms, an
office, a garage, and a media room, frame views
of the surroundings while preserving privacy.
Sustainability was central to decision-making
throughout the design and construction process:
the teak boards used were salvaged to avoid felling
additional trees, and the roof was tiled with solar
panels that generate energy for the residents and
send surplus energy back to the grid.

GREEN SHED 2010

The Finnish-designed Green Shed is conceived
as an innovative combination of a small-scale
greenhouse and invisible tool storage, and yet its
modular and prefabricated character allows it to
transform into a house or a cabin with a gross floor
area of up to 110 ft^2 (10 m^2). The structure, designed
for the horticulture company Kekkilä Garden, is
made of Finnish pine and toughened safety glass
throughout, rendering it simple yet sturdy. The gable-
roof shape imbues it with a sense of romanticism,
while its steep pitch has the practical benefit
of displacing snowfall. The use of glass and the
diminutive size make the shed appear whimsical
or dreamlike. It is an escape from reality while being
highly connected with the natural surroundings
in all directions. Glass windows and glass panels
in larger structures often frame a viewpoint or
panorama, making us a knowing and, thus, distant
observer, but in the case of Green Shed, we are
completely immersed in the environment. Total
transparency gives the illusion of tranquility and
silence, as clutter, mundane objects, and confusion
are eliminated from view. Nothing is superfluous;
everything is necessary; and our presence inside
the shed becomes a pared-back experience as
we look out into nature, seeing and feeling only
what is fundamental.

VICTORIAN REMIX   2017

The Victorians might be known as the inventors of leisure time, but their take on nineteenth-century domestic architecture was far from light-flooded or luxurious. Today, London still carries the heritage of terraced houses from this era across nearly all districts. The original house was the same in this case, suffering from tight spaces and little light on the first floor. Situated on a typically narrow South London plot, the architects decided to remove the lower rear facade and replace it with a fully glazed box. A striking intervention which dramatically increased the availability of light and allowed for a new spatial flow connecting indoor activities to continous views of the garden. A new basement was excavated to allow a swimming pool and steam room to be installed. The intervention sounds substantial and has a considerable effect on the airiness and light within the transformed spaces, but the use of glass helped to minimize the interference with the heritage of the original home while creating a maximal result. As a result of being only 18 ft (5.5 m) wide, the original house had felt uninviting and disjointed. Working with glass allowed the architects to connect the different floors and spaces of the structure simply by shifting around, or remixing, certain aspects rather than adding a full-blown extension, thus keeping the Victorian blueprint alive while opening and thus modernizing the facade and transforming the experience of living in the house for the residents.

SHOKAN HOUSE   2015

In theory, this house could be placed virtually anywhere; taken out of its context, no site-specific hint or local material would give away that it is situated above the Ashokan Reservoir, about two hours' drive from Manhattan. A half-mile (0.8-km) gravel road and a manmade pond further separate the imposing structure and the pristine surrounding nature. From the outside, one first notices the sturdiness of reinforced and exposed concrete, black steel, and reflective glass. Once inside, however, the entire volume opens onto the nature reserve beyond, with majestic views that can be enjoyed in every direction. Everything is built around

the concept of contrast: inside, the soberness continues with stainless-steel counters, perforated at times, walnut cabinetry, and black surfaces here and there; outside, the velvety tops of fir, spruce, oak, and birch spread their soft green aura across the entire valley, a spectacle to be observed in the changing light and weather conditions every single day. The glass facade allows the austere design and the lush scenery to permeate each other rather than to simply coexist. One extreme nurtures the other, so that, in the end, it is clear that Shokan House is precisely where it needs to be.

GLASS-BLOCK MICRO HOUSE 2020

Sitting on a small 194-ft^2 (18-m^2) plot in a narrow alleyway in Ho Chi Minh City, this urban micro-house was originally built from traditional bricks that created a claustrophobic feel with limited light within the modestly sized interiors. As well as renovating and improving the property, the new owners wanted to add a second function to the living space to accommodate their start-up leather fashion business. To increase the level of daylight in the interiors, the architects proposed an innovative and ambitious change: two of the exterior walls were replaced by glass-block facades. The result is well executed and enhances the living conditions, and indeed the entire street, as the house becomes a warm beacon in the evenings, shining a light on the neighborhood. The first floor also integrates two glass vitrines directly inserted into the facade, which function as a small shopfront. This way, the living room doubles as a reception space for the shop. On the second floor, a smaller bedroom and bathroom furnished in a traditional style with a contemporary twist find their place. On the third floor, a terrace is added to the layout of the rooms, together with a pergola that wraps around the building to provide planting space and strengthen the relationship between indoor and outdoor living.

GLASS PAVILION   2018

Situated high in Spain's Gorafe Desert, a semi-arid region northeast of Granada, Glass Pavilion proposes a possible future for glass dwellings. Conceived as boutique holiday retreat and a showcase for a new type of glass with superior thermic abilities, it only features essentials: a bedroom, a living area, and a bathroom. From its remote location, the innovative and photogenic property embodies the spirit of discovery. Resting on top of a hill, it appears to have been dropped from space. The glazed unit, made up of three separate modules, sits under a reflective metal roof that flows around the top of the glass. The roof and plinth form a narrow 360° veranda extending beyond the glass core. The modest outside area

can be closed off with textile curtains that protect the terrace from overheating and offer guests shade and privacy. The structural glass walls are triple-glazed panes with an invisible coating that filters solar radiation, ensuring a comfortable living environment in extreme climatic conditions. Inside, a labyrinth of myriad light reflections animates the view. At the center of the dwelling is a small bathroom with opaque walls and doors that stand in distinct contrast to the transparency of the rest of the volume. The mirror-clad canopy roof, plinth, and glass core, reflect back the dramatic skies and topography on all sides, merging them in a series of repeating geometric patterns and minimizing the visual impact of the pavilion from a distance.

ENGAWA HOUSE   2019

Little hints at the existence of a fully glazed
volume on this particular site. Instead, a slatted-
wood box appears on the horizon between two
small, rocky bays on the Pacific Ocean coastline.
The house and ocean are hidden from each
other by thick, bushy vegetation, even though
the structure is elevated on tilted red metal stilts.
Beneath the stilts, a shaded terrace provides
outside space for the family. The single-story
volume is wrapped in slatted sheets of wood that
provide intimacy and seclusion inside. An enclosed
walkway between the glazed box and the wooden
paneling ensures the effect of an airy sunshade
rather than claustrophobia. This edging strip running
around the entire building is called "engawa" in
Japanese and gives the house its name. It creates
an intermediate, liminal area that is neither entirely
outside nor part of the open-plan interior living area.
The regular pattern of the wooden slates throws
eye-catching parallel stripes of shade and reflections
across the glazed window panels. The internal
space is relatively compact and cabin-like, even
though it is arranged in a minimal contemporary
style. Residents can look out onto the dramatic
natural setting while remaining near invisible and
protected from the heat and glare of the sun.

FARNSWORTH HOUSE   1951

Just outside Chicago, in a 10-acre (4-ha) secluded wooded site with the Fox River to the south, a glass pavilion embodies Ludwig Mies van der Rohe's concept of a functional relationship between a house and the surrounding nature. The one-room weekend retreat, originally built for medical doctor Edith Farnsworth, has a total area of 1,500 ft^2 (140 m^2) and follows the International Style, which is defined by an emphasis on volume over mass, the use of lightweight, mass-produced, industrial materials, rejection of all ornament and color, repetitive modular forms, and the use of flat surfaces, typically alternating with areas of glass. The structure consists of eight I-shaped steel columns that are load-bearing, yet present only a minimal intervention into the natural environment, allowing the base of the pavilion to float 5 ft 3 in. (1.6 m) above the ground. As the style requests, all spaces between the steel columns are filled by floor-to-ceiling windows encompassing the entire house. The glass in this context is imbued with an important social meaning, being one of the first completely glazed dwellings it challenged notions about privacy and created a new trend and status symbol. Mies was convinced that seeing nature from the inside of the house would enhance the experience by giving it a frame and vantage point: "When you see nature through the glass walls of Farnsworth House, it gets a deeper meaning than [from] outside," he explained.

GLASS VILLA ON THE LAKE   2018

Mecanoo's glass villa is an oasis within an oasis. Rather than standing beside the lake, the structure sits directly on the water, becoming a part of it. Situated in Gloucestershire in Southwest England, a bridge connects the house with the access road, curving through tall trees that hide the plot from view and were preserved throughout construction. Large floor-to-ceiling windows with glass corners in most rooms allow seamless views of the lake, which is further enhanced by the open plan layout, ensuring the views are available from every part of the house. The highly reflective glazed facade captures the movement of the trees and the clouds, and, in what appears to be a reciprocal arrangement, the house is reflected onto the glimmering surface of the lake for much of the day. Two outdoor terraces hover alongside lush aquatic plants, giving the impression of a floating garden and strengthening the connection between the lake and the land. Another outstanding feature of the structure is its large central atrium, which connects all three floors through a staircase, and glazed light channels that flood the interior with daylight. Below the water level, the atrium connects to a basement, which accommodates a cinema, and on the top level, it opens onto the rooftop garden offering impressive views of the landscape in all directions.

THE CONSERVATORY   2017

This industrial reinterpretation of contemporary African architecture was conceived to embrace its surroundings on an impressive 87-acre (35-hectare) site outside South Africa's administrative capital Pretoria. The focal point of the building is the double-height glass conservatory that appears as a house inside a house, sitting between two large solid wings. Black steel window frames figure across the whole structure to create continuity between the conservatory, the only fully glazed component, and the exposed brick-clad outer sections. Alternating opaque and translucent corrugated sheets form a gable roof above the generous communal space. A centrally placed table is the main element in the minimally furnished room, accentuating the openness created by the glass. The front and back facades can be electronically opened to connect the dining area to the outdoors, with impressive views of the adjacent grasslands, dams, and rock embankment. Glazed double doors further expand and connect the room to the side functions, which house the sleeping areas. Floor-to-ceiling glazed interior partitions with black steel frames continue the conservatory style more domestically and practically. Extensive thought has also been given to airflow and thermic balance in all weather conditions, and off-grid systems, including solar panels, render the dwelling sustainable and independent.

MIRADOR HOUSE   2021

A house located in the Ecuadorian forest needed extending, and time constraints led the architects to devise an industrially prefabricated building solution. The glass and metal single-story rectangular unit floats above the hillside to reduce any impact on the soil and ecosystems of the site. Floor-to-ceiling glazing has been installed throughout, offering immersive views of the lush vegetation, creating a tropical forest cabin with a sophisticated and minimal design. The triple exposure creates a luminous atmosphere, amplified by reflections of the surrounding trees bouncing back and forth between the glass panels. A black steel frame outlines and supports the structure. On the inside, the same material is used for fixtures and fittings, including storage and a large fireplace; the dark surfaces enter the dialogue between neon tubes, the primary artificial light source, the natural light, and the all-around glazing. At the heart of the space, a plywood unit divides the room and houses an expansive kitchen. Another plywood storage unit separates the extension from the original building, which contains three bedrooms and a bathroom. The new volume allows the owners to enjoy a generous space in what was formerly a small house and marvel at the breathtaking forest surrounding them.

THE HUDSON VALLEY GLASS HOUSE   1967

In 1967, in New York's Westchester County, architect Robert Fitzpatrick built a modern home with extensive steel-framed floor-to-ceiling glazing. Arriving at the entrance to the house, only the upper floor is visible, the public areas of lounge and living space, while the excavated lower level, containing bedrooms and a family room, remains hidden from view while offering the same luminous prospects onto the green lawns and trees of the plot. Seen from the side, the six large rectangular glass window panels of the two floors, stacked on top of one another in rows of three, impress with their modernist simplicity. A set of long white curtains hangs beside each pane to provide privacy when needed and create a striking aesthetic when they are all used simultaneously. Each room in the property features at least one full wall of floor-to-ceiling glass, and the living room benefits from triple exposure. A pool to the rear of the building and the surrounding trees are reflected onto the surface of the windows, animating the geometric structure. In 2001, the interior of the house was remodeled by interior designer Magdalena Keck with the brief to render the dialogue with the outdoors paramount; for example, considering how objects within the rooms would look from outside alongside their aesthetics and function inside.

HIDDEN PAVILION   2016

Conceived as a place for contemplation, Hidden Pavilion sits in a forest clearing in the municipality of Las Rozas, just over 12 miles (20 km) from Madrid. While the fully glazed reflective shell dissolves into the terrain, five red chimney-like lightwells stand out against the green, catching the eye from afar and recalling the domes that define the Arab-Norman Church of San Cataldo in Sicily. In fact, the house exudes ceremonial simplicity. Despite the industrial appearance of its construction, the building has been embedded into its surroundings with care and respect; plants grow freely through its terraces, passing through specially built openings. The upper-level facade is carefully angled to allow for the growth of a 200-year-old oak tree. The juxtaposition between rigid shapes, neutral glass surfaces, and reflections of the organic vegetation creates a tranquil atmosphere. Only three materials have been utilized: rusted steel for the structural beams; glass to cover and expose the entire building; and cherry wood for the simple interiors, all of which combine to create a distinct sense of poetry. Honest in its straightforward design and simple in its lack of ornament, the Pavilion is dedicated to observing the natural world. Here, the residents can feel a part of the changing seasons.

THE ROUND HOUSE   1968

The shape of this impressive dwelling is an idealistic yet practical solution to an essentially romantic problem. Richard Foster desired all-around views of the spectacular green dip on the plot he had discovered to build a home for his family while not wanting to impose a large structure on the landscape. So he devised a raised circular house set on a cylindrical base about 12 ft (3.7 m) off the ground, supported by stones, and walled in glass to allow 360-degree viewpoints. Specialist engineering techniques developed in Germany have been employed to render the unusual structure sound, together with local Connecticut steel and stone from the Dolomites in Italy. The futuristic shape is balanced with a vernacular building style and a sense of modernity in the interior. The plan may appear dated today, as one needs to move around the house to appreciate the views rather than simply turn on the spot, as is often the case in fully glazed buildings today, but it is precisely this that renders the house special. It is a place from which to meditate and observe with discretion. Intimate domesticity is linked to the materials used; none stands in contrast with the glass or structure, but all gently support the bold shape. The effect is mirrored on the lower patio, which sits directly underneath the living area and offers an identical panorama without glass walls.

GLASS HOUSE   1952

Glass House was the first residence designed by Lina Bo Bardi to be constructed. Built as a home for herself and her husband, the journalist and museum director Pietro Maria Bardi, a meeting place for artist friends, and a space to work, it does not lack in lightness or geometry. The plot is located in one of the most elevated areas in Morumbi, in Brazil's largest city of São Paulo, which features lush tropical vegetation, and is well chosen for the double exposure to nature proposed by Bo Bardi's architecture. From the inside of Glass House, it is possible to observe nature twice: first, through the glazed canopy on stilts, a prime motif of the Modern Movement, and then, through the glazed courtyard, where a tree grows in the center.

The glass sections were conceived with public functions in mind, probably as much for show as for sharing the breathtaking views. In this case, the glass is not contrasted with warm materials inside, but simply completed by Bo Bardi's designs, such as the system of metal shelves that at once highlight and obstruct the view without contradiction. The more private functions are nestled at the back of the house, constructed from brick and without stilts, using a more vernacular and intimate vocabulary. Considered to be one of the most important examples of twentieth-century Latin American architecture, the couple's former home now houses an institute dedicated to their work.

LOS TERRENOS   2016

Monterrey is the second largest city in Mexico and a bustling center for business and industry. In the green mountains to its southwest, architect Tatiana Bilbao has designed a forest refuge. It is composed of three volumes that respond to different needs, the largest of which houses the public functions of kitchen and living space. Entirely clad in glass, it stands out visually and conceptually for the one-way mirrors that allow the house to be absorbed by the forest. Even though the space is conceived for public gatherings, privacy is maintained as guests can enjoy the view without being seen from outside–a rare feature in residential glass architecture. The facade of Los Terrenos is a homage to the light and vegetation of the lush forest, which are reflected onto the surface. On the terrace, too, centerstage has been given to nature and the existing trees, which have been considered and accomodated rather than cut down: clay-tile-masonry lets water seep into the ground to nurture their roots. The gable roof mimics the shape of a traditional house, evocatively confirming that the architectural deconstruction into different parts is gentle and familiar rather than cold and modernist. In fact, only the main dwelling features glass as a building material. The sleeping structure has been conceived in clay for warmth, and a third volume, constructed from wood, is to follow.

VILLA MOSCA BIANCA 2019

Seen from above, Villa Mosca Bianca appears as an island on the Piedmont shore of Lake Maggiore. The lake, the second largest in Italy and southern Switzerland, is famous for its serenity and provides a perfect setting for luxury tourism. The structure of the house consists of three floating concrete slabs stacked on top of each other, held together by slender pilasters, and enclosed by glass. The layout ensures that each of the four bedrooms benefits from panoramic views of the pine forest and the expanse of the lake. The building is defined by a complex, organically shaped facade of rounded glass that wraps around the entire building without forming a single right angle. The irregular shape of each layer creates a system of terraces across the stacked volume, offering easy access to outdoor space. A central open-air garden extends over two floors cutting through the volume with sinuous glass walls that reflect the interior and exterior back and forth. The glazing provides natural light and passive ventilation throughout the villa, with solar panels, heat pumps, and a rainwater collection system contributing to the energy efficiency of this large glass dwelling. Rough and exposed details of natural stone and other unpolished materials inside create a textural contrast with the sleek, meditative omnipresence of glass.

HOUSE IN GARRISON 2008

Located in Garrison, a rural getaway in New York state, this extensive house comprises two distinct fully glazed rectangular volumes aligned at right angles to capture different views of the Hudson River and the mountains in the distance. The clients wanted a second home inspired by the great modernist works of Mies van der Rohe and Philip Johnson while avoiding the problems these predominantly glass houses posed, especially concerning controlling temperature and ventilation. Separating the volumes permits each space to be heated as needed while mechanical systems, including a geothermal heat pump and in-slab radiant heating, supply sustainable warmth, an elegant and efficient solution to the thermal challenges of glass constructions. The lower part of the open plan structure unites the kitchen and living space, offering impressive views of the waterfront, while the bedrooms are housed in the volume above, which dramatically cantilevers beyond the footprint of the first floor. The glass has been used as both a stylistic and a practical device, reflecting the necessities and desires of the clients. A generous roof light floods the impressive entryway with sunlight, providing perfect conditions for the owners' collection of tropical trees. A band of translucent glass panes encircles the top of the lower volume and the bottom of the upper volume, emphasizing the connection between the two levels and diffusing daylight as it enters the house. At night, the whole building lights up, creating the impression of an immense minimalist sculpture.

SOLO HOUSE II   2017

The Solo Houses project is a series of luxury holiday dwellings in the pristine forest of the mountainous region of Matarraña in the north of Spain, each designed by different architects. Brussels-based studio OFFICE Kersten Geers David Van Severen developed the second of fifteen homes to be built. Their proposal is a circular, predominantly glass structure with a 148-ft (45-m) diameter that seems to merge with the landscape through reflections created by the unusual shape. The circular roof is supported by four rows of eight columns, delineating four fully glazed indoor living areas. These spaces can be opened entirely to the elements, thanks to glass curtain facades, allowing them to communicate with the outdoor terraces that constitute the remainder of the circular construction. A large garden fills the middle of the structure, ensuring residents can enjoy seamless views of nature in all directions and offering a more intimate space to meet and spend time together. Most of the 0.4-acre (1,600-m²) plot is dedicated to the patio and swimming pool, with the living room, master bedroom, and guest bedroom making up the interior space. The resort is not connected to any services, so the dwelling is entirely off-grid and relies on solar panels for heating and electricity. On the roof, tanks and a filtration system purify rainwater to drinking quality. The poetry of OFFICE's design lies in the combination of an unusual form and its luxurious execution, allowing users to connect with nature in comfort.

MAISON DE VERRE   1932

Despite being concealed in an enclosed courtyard in the 7th arrondissement of Paris, the Maison de Verre is a well-known piece of early modernist architecture. Tasked with designing a family home and surgery for Dr. Jean Dalsace and his wife Annie, the architects were forced to build the glass box underneath the third-floor apartment of a resident who refused to leave the original nineteenth-century building, thus creating the need for extra innovation and creativity. A steel skeleton

made from a system of industrial pillars and beams supports the old structure, eliminating the need for load-bearing walls in the new house and allowing total programmatic flexibility. Closing the steel frame, a grid of translucent square glass bricks floods the interiors with diffused daylight while providing privacy for patients and residents. Frame construction also enabled the architects to play with ceiling heights, a flexibility they took advantage of to create a spectacular double-height grand salon on

the second floor, as well as subtle changes in level that divide the space without the need for walls. There is a mechanical intricacy in the fixtures and fittings inside the home, including sliding, folding, and rotating glass and metal screens and a wheel-operated system of hopper vents that allows fresh air in without visually impacting the facade. At night, thanks to external floodlamps, the interior lights up as though on a sunny day.

BOATHOUSE STUDIO   2010

What may appear as a conventional glass box in a stunning location is, in reality, an intricately composed technical device. The lakeside setting on Stony Lake in central Ontario, Canada plays its part, but there is more to this once humble boathouse, which has been transformed into a photographer's studio. The raison d'être of the structure is to maximize the availability of natural light, hence the transparent facade. The curtain walls glazed in low-iron glass allow the photographer to produce images unobtainable in a conventional studio; the north light flooding the double-height structure makes for unparalleled natural illumination. Together with the panoramic backdrop of the surrounding nature, it is the perfect photographer's studio. The interiors are kept sharply white, minimal, and versatile enough to accommodate living space needs, while remaining photogenic at all times. Sliding panes in the glass skin—9.8 ft (3 m) wide on the first floor and 4.9 ft (1.5 m) wide on the mezzanine floor—allow the space to open up and allow natural ventilation, an additional asset for thermic control in summer. An automated system of blinds, a white roof, and a strategically placed hedgerow garden protect the studio from overheating. The whole structure is hosted on a granite plinth, which disappears in low light and makes the whole form seem to float over the lake at night.

SUMMER HOUSE 2016

Between a pine forest and the open sea, Summer House is a quintessential Finnish summer dwelling. It has been kept consciously small and as simple as possible; the expansive views and the wilderness of the site impress rather than the 969-ft^2 (90-m^2) size of the residence. Nature has been respected in the building plans. Firstly, the narrow construction runs parallel to the shoreline, creating a protective mass against the predominant winds. Secondly, the house is heated by geothermal energy. Thirdly, Summer House has made minimal impact on the landscape in which it sits. In terms of aesthetics, the wave-shaped roof imitates and befriends the sea and the rocks while extending over the structure to provide shelter from the sun and rain. The wave-shaped roof begets the shape of the glazing, which follows the same wavelike motion and gives the house an extremely modern yet organic appearance. By maximizing the glass surface and minimizing interruptions between single panels, the outer shell functions as a canvas for reflections created by the sun and surrounding landscape. On the outside, the wooden roof and terrace with in-situ cast concrete base are the only opaque additions apart from the load-bearing frame and its bracing, which have steel elements. Otherwise, the pavilion remains impressively transparent, offering uninterrupted views of the scenery from inside the house. The interiors have been furnished using oak, steel, limestone, and copper in simple, functional shapes to blend silently with the colors of the ever-present landscape.

LIBRARY HOUSE   2016

A space to read and think in was the client's brief for the steep hilltop site in the Atlantic rainforest of Vinhedo in São Paulo. In response to the topography, the structure sits on three different levels, the only provision that divides the open-plan space into minimally separate living spaces. None of this can be seen from street level. There, only the concrete roof appears as an enormous, inanimate viewing platform, which is, in fact, its function. Below, the entirely glazed house rests on a substantial concrete base that was cast on-site in a single day. The facade is divided into an irregular grid of steel-framed window panes, which invites an air of art deco into the otherwise tropical Brazilian modernism. The rectangular panes frame and fragment views and reflections of the dense vegetation surrounding the property, lending it an ethereal appearance. The lush greenery appears to flow through the windows softening the severe yet elegant forms of the structure and allowing it to merge into the forest. Recalling a greenhouse or a pavilion more than a traditional home, the retreat is defined not only by its architectural style and location, but by the client's desire for a perfect place to read and contemplate nature.

HOFMANN HOUSE   2018

While many glass houses surrounded by nature are designed to blend in, this house is built to stand out. Its elongated, rigid shape and the bright white of the roof and flooring cut sharply across the panorama of bushy treetops and soft blue sky. The structure is dominated by a T-shaped roof that covers a glass box below and expands into a spacious rooftop terrace above. The roof is shaped to protect one side of the glazed building from being viewed from the outside, allowing residents to observe without being observed. Seclusion is also provided by the sloped site and interior aluminum paneling that envelops the box containing the private functions. The other side of the entirely glazed house opens onto the terrace and pool, which run the length of the house. To separate the structure visually from its surroundings, it has been built on a plinth, which introduces the minimal, white color regime that extends over the entire plan and makes little to no disturbance to the glazing, which is framed without appearing weighed down. The watery reflections of the pool and the surrounding trees animate the generous glass surfaces. Materials such as steel and marble have been chosen to maximize the light diffusion inside the house, accentuated by neon-tube lighting bouncing off the reflective surface of the glass.

PAM AND PAUL'S HOUSE   2016

This ambitious and creative house overlooks an oak grove in the Santa Cruz Mountains in Cupertino above Silicon Valley. It is an almost entirely glass-walled home of cubic shape and considerable size. While the interior space is flooded with dappled daylight, it also benefits from a dense tree canopy that protects it from the heat of direct sunbeams. The combination of all-around glazing and rounded corners renders the structure light, making it appear to float within the dense oak grove. Two thick, tree-like columns support the main program. Inside, the impact of the rounded glass is even more potent as some sections have been mirrored, giving an otherworldly feeling and creating a soft and comfortable distance from the stress of the outside world. The living room, the office, and the kitchen are sunken below the concrete floor, maximizing the field of vision. On the ceiling above, integrated LED lighting lines follow the outline of the furnished spaces underneath, and when lit, their reflections form a continuous dialogue with the rounded glass walls. Strong material choices, such as Chinese pistachio, concrete, and zinc, create a pleasant contrast to the liquidity of the overall design, which is palpable both from the outside and inside.

SMALL HOUSE   2000

The high cost of land in the dense city center of Tokyo is reflected in the creative living solutions found in its architecture. The previous owners had not full exploited this 646-ft^2 (60-m^2) plot in the Aoyama district of the city, whose first floor occupied merely 388 ft^2 (36 m^2) of the available space. Kazuyo Sejima has designed a rectangular tower, allowing the upper floors to extend to the plot's full potential, expanding in the middle and tapering in toward the roof. To enable this intervention, the glass panels are placed on a diagonal, creating an asymmetric shape that contrasts with the neighboring residences. The irregular glazing creates interesting viewpoints and reflections of the neighboring trees. A load-bearing metal structure in the middle of the building supports and integrates a plexiglass-wrapped spiral staircase from which all four floors can be accessed and that doubles as a luminous shaft of light, especially at night. In addition, the staircase shaft enacts thermic control by moving warm air upward and expelling it toward the top. To provide privacy, the fully transparent floor-to-ceiling window panels have been wrapped with skins of varying transparency, ranging from mild protection to fully opaque zinc sheeting, depending on their relationship to the neighboring buildings. By contrast, the north and west fronts overlooking the gardens of an adjacent temple have been left completely uncovered.

WIMBLEDON HOUSE   1969

In many ways, this modest single-story house in Wimbledon, southwest London, designed by architects Su and Richard Rogers is an early European iteration of Californian Modernism, which began in the 1950s. It was built for Richard Rogers's parents, with noble intentions regarding the broader ecosystem of British housing, then in crisis. The idea was to develop a house using a new prefabricated construction system that could be replicated at a low cost with readily available materials that could be quickly and easily assembled "avoiding the bad weather," as Richard Rogers said. Bright yellow steel frames are aligned and sealed with full-height glazing at each end, while the partitions on the inside can be reconfigured as desired. The large glass panels create a visual continuity that extends the vibrant ambience propagated by Rogers's use of colors and shapes into the outdoors, embracing the garden and the absent walls. Formerly known as The Rogers House or 22 Parkside, Wimbledon House is visibly a precursor to the postmodern Centre Pompidou in Paris, made predominantly of glass and steel, and inaugurated in 1977. In recent years, Wimbledon House has been used by Harvard students as a residence and base from which to conduct research.

VARANDA HOUSE   2007

Located within a typical Brazilian garden setting, Varanda House is reminiscent of a particular type of tropical modernism, the style associated with Sri Lankan architect Geoffrey Bawa. The client was the granddaughter of architect Sergio Bernardes, who also practiced tropical modernism, and she wanted a dwelling that reflected her grandfather's architectural vision. The simplicity of the house is striking and accentuates the richness of the landscape it sits within. The rectangular glass volume is constructed on stilts to accommodate seasonal flooding, creating a minimally invasive, elegant aesthetic. The structure is composed of a steel skeleton, which is fully glazed with sliding floor-to-ceiling panels on both sides, making an entirely permeable living space that flows seamlessly into the surrounding garden. The corrugated steel roof includes an important feature: a central roof light, 2 ft (0.6 m) wide and 79 ft (24 m) long, that runs across the entire length of the ceiling, supplying the living spaces with an additional natural light source as the sun moves across the sky. Weather-resistant materials were chosen to protect the structure from degradation caused by the humid sea air of the region. Easy-to-assemble and low-cost materials allowed the structure of Varanda House to be constructed in just fifteen days. Warm wooden fittings and minimal furniture communicate subtle comfort, sitting between the modernist rigidity and the tropical vegetation visible throughout, thanks to the continuous glazing.

VILLA KOGELHOF 2013

It is unusual for architects to transform and engineer the land they build on beforehand. In this project, however, that transformation cost more than the actual building. The site is a 62-acre (25-hectare) estate near Kamperland, a village in the Dutch province of Zeeland, and permission was only given to build if the land, part of a designated ecological zone, was returned to its pre-agricultural state. This involved planting over 70,000 trees and creating a large pond for migratory birds. When the trees mature, the house will be lost to view. Conceived as an energy-neutral dwelling, the home comprises two stacked stories, one below ground and one floating above the land to minimize its footprint on the ecosystem. Uninterrupted curtain walls enclose the upper volume, allowing spectacular views over the landscape and contributing to the self-sufficient intention with an innovative ventilation system that balances the climate inside the large villa. A transparent water roof allows natural light to penetrate the underground level, which houses the entrance, extensive garage, storage, and workspace. The open-plan living space above is minimally furnished to ensure that the views are unobstructed and the abundant daylight flows freely. At night, when different sections of the long rectangular volume are illuminated, and in winter, when everything is covered in snow, the glass facade reveals its full effect.

FLIP HOUSE   2013

Flip House, located in northern California, is dominated by dynamic transparency. Beyond the fully glazed facade, glass is used for interior partitions and exterior railings. The brief was to remodel and make sense of a confused existing house, and the architect incorporated a strong concept of movement in the transformation plan, flipping the main facade away from the street toward the garden. Three vertical panels of prism-shaped windows push in and out of the custom-designed facade, animating the sunlight and reflections as they hit it, creating a sense of multidirectional movement. In the interior, perforated steel allows the daylight pouring in to punctuate the shaft of the new rear staircase that now links all floors of the dwelling, replacing the original disconnected staircases. Rather than being closed off, the spaces are now open and separated or connected only by glass walls, floor-to-ceiling height in the case of the bedroom, and half-height in the main living space and kitchen. Only the bedrooms, now orientated to face the street, have been hidden from passersby. In its new iteration, light entering the house from the garden flows freely through all floors and is reflected back and forth by the glass railings and glazed walls. Together with the minimal interior design, this creates a pleasant, bright, and free living space, with views out to the city and the Bay.

TOWER HOUSE   2012

Only a two-hour drive from New York City, the
Catskills is a popular weekend destination for
New Yorkers, known for its unspoiled countryside
and the wide variety of outdoor leisure activities it
offers. The architects conceived a stacked layout
on a tiny footprint for this vacation property to
avoid disturbing the woodlands any more than
necessary. There are three bedrooms with en suite
bathrooms, one on top of the other in a single,
glazed tower with the kitchen, living space, and
a roof terrace positioned at the very top, creating
a "treetop aerie" that looks across to the rugged
terrain of the Catskill Mountains. The extensive
living space features ribbon windows that run the
entire length of the room to maximize the panoramic
views. Interestingly, only the staircase is fully glazed,
meaning the bright yellow stair is visible from the
outside, radiating joy and rendering the structure
less severe. The other rooms in the house feature
selective floor-to-ceiling windows, interspersed
with dark green, back-painted glass panels, which
help to camouflage the house by reflecting the
surrounding woods and de-materializing its form
among the lush treetops. At dusk, tiny lights set
into stair rail glow, mimicking fireflies twinkling in
the woods.

VIGGSÖ   2016

Constraints on a project, perhaps a restricted budget or tight schedule, may seem frustrating but can often lead to greater clarity and focus in the finished work. In the case of Viggsö, the architects had to respond to the natural requirements of the site—the largest island of the Stockholm archipelago—and a limited budget. These two factors combined to produce a light construction that would not impact too heavily on its rocky situation, characterized by dense undergrowth and slim pine trees swaying in the strong winds. Opting for a timber-frame structure reminiscent of Walter Segal's self-build revolution, they designed a solid yet delicate system with a simple and symmetrical floor plan. The simplicity of the proposal allows the all-around glazing to become the protagonist of the holiday retreat, framing craggy outcrops, patches of forest, and the maritime coast, sometimes sliced through by the timber diagonals of the house. The natural timber and floor-to-ceiling glass accentuate the Nordic color palette of lichen-covered rocks, dark greens, and deep blue waters. Divided into three equal sections, the house measures a modest 860 ft^2 (80 m^2), comprising the master bedroom, the living area with a mezzanine floor to host guests and children, and finally, a large terrace to enjoy the outdoors fully. The roof changes from corrugated steel to plexiglass in the section above the deck, deepening the impression of transparency and lightness with which the house sits on its slender stilts.

STAHL HOUSE   1960

Stahl House, completed in 1960 for Buck and Carlotta Stahl, overlooks Los Angeles from the Hollywood Hills. It is #22 of the *Arts & Architecture* magazine Case Study House Program, whose agenda was to experiment with and normalize replicable building techniques that used modern industrial materials, such as glass, in the postwar era. The plan is L-shaped, enclosing a pool, with narrow beams holding up an overshooting flat roof made of metal. Floor-to-ceiling windows on three sides offer dramatic views of the city of Los Angeles that define the house. The concept here is not to get away from the city, to connect with nature, or to hide in exclusivity, but to be a perfect modern part of the city. The glamour of the structure, portrayed in countless photographs —most famously in 1960 by Julius Shulman, who placed two women against the glimmering evening lights of Los Angeles—and films, lies in its panoramic view of the city. Without the modernity of Los Angeles, the postwar promise of the glazed cantilever would not have any appeal. With that backdrop, however, Stahl House promises both a new life and a step back from the domesticity of suburbia. Maybe this is why the glossy structure looks so good in photographs and film sets; they do not have to live up to the mundane reality of life.

HOUSE WITH ONE WALL   2007

The feature that gives its name to this building is not the all-round glazing but the single concrete load-bearing wall that folds and breaks into different directions, like a folded piece of paper, in order to stand freely and securely on its edge, dividing the structure into two separate homes. Together with the glass envelope that closes the two volumes along the outside, the wall dictates the shape of the living spaces. Each floor houses one long open-plan room, with services hidden by folds in the wall. The use of glass is substantial; next to reinforced concrete, it is the primary material and gives the structure its distinct identity, and only the bathrooms have opaque elements, although drapes can be pulled across to provide privacy. Located in a semi-urban area of Zurich, the extensive floor-to-ceiling glass cladding produces an unexpected transparency that remains undisturbed by other living units close by, with views from both halves of the building concentrating instead on the modest garden and the vast horizon beyond. By framing the mundane surroundings, the glass provides a reassuringly domestic panorama that contrasts with the otherwise raw and industrial aesthetic of the concrete walls, ceilings, and floors.

TJURPANNAN HOUSE   2022

This coastal cabin benefits from stunning views from its isolated location at the edge of Tjurpannan Nature Reserve in western Sweden and matches the austerity of its surroundings. The design for the structure responds to the rocky landscape, which has been shaped by exposure to wind and the adjacent coast of the North Sea. Respecting the topography, the cabin is built on a grid of stilts, anchored into the rock through slim iron rods only where necessary. This principle of bare necessity elegantly repeats throughout the cabin. The two long sides of the volume feature floor-to-ceiling glazing, bringing nature into the home, where it is echoed by stained wood-clad walls and ceilings. Darker, tarred wood is used for the exterior structural elements and frames the reflections of the surrounding trees on the glazed surfaces, rendering the body of the house almost invisible from the outside, helping to camouflage it. Apart from the elaborate glazed side panels, this practical house is defined by a standardized grid and realized with rustic materials typically found in local hardware stores. The gable roof with corrugated steel sheets completes this simple yet perfectly executed combination of luxurious camping, the romance of trees, and the wildness of the landscape.

KRAMLICH RESIDENCE AND COLLECTION 2015

Fascinated by Herzog & de Meuron's Dominus Winery in Napa Valley, Pam and Dick Kramlich commissioned a state-of-the-art residence to house their video and media art collection. Initially, the architects proposed a plan featuring a transparent pavilion with curved glass walls to be used as a projection surface, allowing images to merge with the surrounding landscape. However, the construction evolved over the years, and the final home takes a different form. The reflective asymmetric glass pavilion is connected, via a rotunda and a glazed spiral staircase to a series of museum-grade gallery spaces suited to the digital medium below, which house most of the Kramlichs' collection. The verdant rolling landscape surrounding the property pervades the spaces above ground, where a series of artworks have been thoughtfully installed, initiating an open-ended dialogue between the glass, the reflections, and the works themselves. To provide different levels of privacy, the architects inserted a mezzanine floor between the lower and upper levels to house a guest bedroom in addition to the master bedroom in the glass pavilion.

DURAVCEVIC – BEN ARI HOUSE   2019

A lot comes together in this cruciform-shaped house located on the North Fork of Long Island in New York. After buying the 20-acre (8-hectare) waterfront site, the clients frequently visited the land for walks with the architects to determine where and in which direction their house should be built. Responding to the site's varied topography, which features forest, coastal brush, beach, and water, they devised a carefully oriented omnidirectional layout with four separate, almost entirely glazed gable volumes, each embracing a different aspect of the landscape rather than following the logic of a single glazed facade. The bedroom spaces, for example, overlook dense woodland, creating an atmosphere of quiet seclusion within them, while the open-plan living areas offer expansive views across a clearing that gently slopes down toward the water contributing to the feeling of spaciousness. Outside, an overhanging zinc-clad roof unites the four wings, protects terraces on all sides, and encloses a courtyard garden at the core of the building. The floor-to-ceiling glass is alive with constantly evolving reflections of the rich and varied landscape, both inside and out, infusing the property with an intimate texture and an explorative and generative spirit.

SQUARE HOUSE   2009

Karuizawa is a resort town in the southeastern part of Nagano Prefecture, frequented for its beautiful landscape, with breathtaking mountain views and cool air even in summer. The hour-long train journey from Tokyo's central station makes the town perfect for a weekend getaway. In this context, architects Makoto Takei and Chie Nabeshima conceived a humble yet impressive glass house that pays tribute to the dense forest surrounding it. The concept of the almost entirely transparent structure takes inspiration from bamboo with its long, slender canes, referenced by the 3-in^2 (75-mm^2) hollow pillars extending through the house to support the floor and roof. Square House features a total of seventy-six aluminum columns, most of which are not actually load-bearing. Some carry services such as water pipes and electric cables, while others play a purely stylistic role. The interior is composed of a single volume with all four elevations opening onto the forest, and the slim columns form gentle partitions along which the different uses of the space are articulated without blocking views of trees outside. Reflections of the columns bounce from the glass, merging with the forest to create a distinctly meditative atmosphere. The square plan sits 26.2 ft (8 m) above the ground and provides almost 900 ft^2 (84 m^2) of living space, which includes a sleeping area, a bathroom, a stainless-steel kitchen with adjacent dining space, and a centrally located fireplace that can be enjoyed from anywhere in the house, just like the view, unobstructed by walls, and inviting continuous dialogue.

HOUSE B   2020

In Biberach an der Riss, in the Upper Swabia region of southern Germany, the need for expansion dictated the form of this ambitious and unusual project. The original site featured a 1970s house built on a steep south-facing slope over three split-level floors, a staircase, and access to a pleasant but underused garden. The extension to the original solid structure presents itself as a steel skeleton entirely clad in glass, providing the family dwelling with a central bright living area that opens onto the garden. Part of the existing house was demolished to allow for more daylight and create a more free-flowing plan, and a staircase that separated spaces from one another was removed. In its place, a new outdoor staircase connects what is now two vertically stacked, self-sufficient residential units, each linked to the original building at ground level. An elevator leads from the garage uphill to the garden level below. The intricate exterior of the building has an industrial character but provides flexibility and comfort for everyday living. The filigree aluminum post-and-beam facade forms three rows of five rectangular windows overlooking the garden and is equipped with a textile sunshade that prevents the floor-to-ceiling glass from overheating without sacrificing the views of the surrounding flora and the valley beyond.

GLASS HOUSE   1949

It is a lesser-known fact that Philip Johnson's Glass House does not stand in isolation but is accompanied by a brick structure, designed to function as a guest house or grant moments of privacy, connected by an underground tunnel from the bathroom. Built as a tribute to his friend and fellow architect Ludwig Mies van der Rohe, who designed some of the pieces of furniture inside, the cubic Glass House is minimal in style and executed with minute attention to symmetry on Johnson's private estate in Connecticut. The location allowed him total control as to who would see or visit the house, thus being able to enjoy almost complete transparency without worry. Views of the landscape conditioned the precise position and orientation of the house. Measuring 55 × 33 ft (16.8 × 10 m), it stands on a promontory overlooking a nearby pond and woodland. Reflections of the trees on the external glass allow the structure to integrate harmoniously with its surroundings. In contrast to many other houses built primarily in glass, the main bedroom is fully visible rather than tucked away in a more intimate setting. Only the bathroom has been hidden from outer view, located in a central cylindric brick tube that cleverly hosts the fireplace on the outside, facing the living room. The same red-brown color continues in the herringbone brick floor, creating a seamlessly organic and monotone material coherency. It is an idyllic yet consequent space, only divided by half-height walnut cabinets and penetrated by the brick cylinder, which extends beyond the roof and interestingly breaks the classically square shapes of transparent modernism.

THE GLASS CABIN   2020

In the Jizera Mountains, a romantically remote 130-year-old cabin surrounded by fir trees lies on the border between the Czech Republic and Poland. The task for the architects was to modernize and open the house toward the beautiful scenery without disturbing its intimate seclusion and rustic aesthetic. They left the original structure untouched as far as possible, apart from cutting through one of its heavy granite walls to connect to the new glass annex, which has been subtly sunken below ground level. The extension is almost entirely glazed, introducing a contemporary openness that invites the landscape to form a prominent part of the interior while introducing a clear separation between the old and the new, a separation complemented by a courageous choice of materials throughout. The furnishings include concrete benches cast in situ and an oven, stove, and wood storage clad in glossy white tiles. A state-of-the-art kitchen island connects to the dining space, where richly dark timber is used on all surfaces. The ceiling is covered with a shiny brass sheet, which gently reflects everything below and creates an increased sense of height below the flat roof. Other additions include the insertion of a striking domed skylight, which allows light to flood into the old part of the house, and a metal staircase, while the original interior walls and floors were restored during the renovation. Where elements could not be salvaged, the structure has been updated with plywood and glass panels that create additional visual highlights and strengthen the connection between the upper and lower floors.

MOUNT STUART GREENHOUSE   2019

No other material would have been able to fulfill the promise of this new extension as successfully as glass. The existing house is a tall nineteenth-century villa in full Italianate style featuring gently sloping hipped roofs and deep overhanging eaves with prominent decorative brackets and wide cornices. Needing to befriend and not overshadow what was already there, the addition brings newness and a distinct identity. The neutral glass walls of the extension complement the red brick walls of the main dwelling, while the two-story glazed volume is structurally held in place by black steel supports, which perfectly echo the black timber veranda without turning into pastiche. The glass walls have been left broadly unobstructed by furniture to meet the client's desire to be "engulfed" by the lush green landscape of their Tasmanian garden. Even the kitchen shelves have been conceived as a metal system that connects to the structural steel beams without adding extra weight or separating the user visually from the outside. While the first floor provides communal space for cooking and living, the floor above—kept to a height that does not compete with the historical roofing—houses the master suite, including a glazed bathroom offering prime views of the garden when enjoying a bath.

COURTYARD HOUSE   2013

The conviction that a new typology of family house was needed led the architects to conceive this courtyard model. It is based on the needs of a single-family household in an urban context and proposes low-density living in a post-sprawl city. It comprises a single-story building with a central outdoor courtyard in the middle that is fully glazed and doubles as an atrium as well as a garden. All living spaces are organized around this primary function and are devised to be private and communal depending on the time of day and need. Walls have been avoided in favor of a continuous loop. Each sleeping space has a storage unit that forms a lateral bracing, WC, and shower that are independent but can also be accessed communally.

The glazing around the internal courtyard, an irregular ten-sided shape composed of wooden floor-to-ceiling frames, invites and promotes transparency across all social dynamics. Together with the glazed outer shell of the volume, the plan promotes light reflections, which dance throughout the building. There is continuity between the outside and inside as views of the river and the surrounding wetlands are reinterpreted through the planting within the courtyard garden, which also acts as a metaphorical and actual breathing space for the tensions that might arise in everyday family life. The courtyard optimizes passive solar gain by allowing light and air inside while anchoring the house to the hillside to maximize thermal insulation.

LOOKING GLASS LODGE   2022

A contemporary cocoon rises unexpectedly from the ground in the woods of Fairlight in East Sussex, in an area of Outstanding Natural Beauty. Thanks to an elaborate metal beam construction, the rectangular volume sits on a slope without impacting the fauna and tree roots below. No trees were felled to make way for the lodge, and preserving the ecology of the site underpinned the project from start to finish. The rectangular structure is clad with western red cedar and provides a frame for the glass facades that extend the gaze uphill and downhill and allow the forest to continue through the house. Self-tinting electrochromic glass that limits overheating and the spill of artificial light has been used to safeguard the local bat population, a protected species. On the inside, the cedar cladding continues, helping to blur the boundary between indoors and outdoors further, although, over time, the outer cladding will weather to a more silver-gray shade. The open-plan interior includes kitchen and dining areas with a living room and a floating, log-burning stove, bringing comfort and understated design into the glazed forest panorama. Birch-plywood timber has been utilized to separate the bedroom and bathroom on the eastern side, benefiting from both full glazing and greater privacy.

HOUSE IN LOS VILOS   2020

The Pritzker-Prize-winning architect Ryue Nishizawa has exploited the sea-view location on the Pacific Ocean to its fullest. Steel columns and glass walls form a rectangular corridor sealed by a board-marked concrete slab roof on the perimeter, allowing for an uninhibited view of the rocky landscape and ocean that dictate the entire existence of the house. The waves of the roof divide the functions of the house; one arch sweeps over the kitchen and dining area, which benefits from the double exposure and opens onto a scenic terrace, while another arch covers the bedroom and en-suite bathroom. The third arch hovers above the sauna room, a wood-paneled, open space with a sunken white bathtub positioned to face the low cliffs being washed over by the ocean waves. The exclusive yet monolithic design of the house stands in stark contrast to the rough wilderness of the natural surroundings, which is the true luxury of the structure. The glass is fundamental in this constellation because it invites the landscape to be an essential part of the architecture. In Los Vilos, no decoration or other distraction is required as long as the eye and the soul can feast on endless views of nature's ever-changing spectacle.

INDEX

Phaidon Press Limited
2 Cooperage Yard
London E15 2QR

Phaidon Press Inc.
65 Bleecker Street
New York, NY 10012

phaidon.com

First published 2023
© 2023 Phaidon Press Limited

ISBN 978 1 83866 750 4

A CIP catalogue record for this book is available
from the British Library and the Library of Congress.

Commissioning Editor: Emilia Terragni
Project Editor: Rosie Pickles
Introduction: Andrew Heid
Project texts: Izabela Anna Moren
Production Controller: Lily Rodgers
Design: Studio Chehade

Printed in China